Born in 1950, Rowan Williams was educated in Swansea (Wales) and Cambridge. He studied for his theology doctorate in Oxford, after which he taught theology in a seminary near Leeds. From 1977 until 1986, he was engaged in academic and parish work in Cambridge, before returning to Oxford as Lady Margaret Professor of Divinity. In 1990 he became a fellow of the British Academy.

In 1992 Professor Williams became Bishop of Monmouth, and in 1999 he was elected as Archbishop of Wales. He became Archbishop of Canterbury in late 2002 with ten years' experience as a diocesan bishop and three as a primate in the Anglican Communion. As archbishop, his main responsibilities were pastoral – whether leading his own diocese of Canterbury and the Church of England, or guiding the Anglican Communion worldwide. At the end of 2012, after ten years as archbishop, he stepped down and moved to a new role as Master of Magdalene College, Cambridge.

Professor Williams is acknowledged internationally as an outstanding theological writer and teacher as well as an accomplished poet and translator. His interests include music, fiction and languages.

D1410471

Meeting God in Mark

Reflections for the Season of Lent

ROWAN WILLIAMS

WESTMINSTER
JOHN KNOX PRESS
LOUISVILLE · KENTUCKY

First published in the United States of America in 2014 by
Westminster John Knox Press
100 Witherspoon Street
Louisville, KY 40202

First published in Great Britain in 2014 by
Society for Promoting Christian Knowledge
36 Causton Street
London SW1P 4ST

14 15 16 17 18 19 20 21 22 23—10 9 8 7 6 5 4 3 2 1

Unless otherwise noted, Scripture quotations are the author's own translation.

Cover design by designpointinc.com
Typeset by Graphicraft Limited, Hong Kong

Library of Congress Cataloging-in-Publication Data is on file at the Library of Congress, Washington, D.C.
ISBN-13: 978-0-664-26052-1

Most Westminster John Knox Press books are available at special quantity discounts when purchased in bulk by corporations, organizations, and special-interest groups. For more information, please e-mail SpecialSales@wjkbooks.com.

Contents

Introduction

I am very much indebted to SPCK for once again being willing to make available to a wider audience what started as a short series of Holy Week talks in Canterbury Cathedral (in 2010). The text has been transcribed from recordings and I have left most of it unaltered, though I have added details to fill out one or two points and occasionally to respond to questions asked after the lectures. It makes no claim whatsoever to reflect current scholarship on Mark's Gospel, though I hope it is not completely at odds with such scholarship. My aim has been simply to offer suggestions for a slow reading of what notoriously feels like a rushed and packed text.

Mark has often – as I note in the first chapter – been rather ignored in the Church's liturgy because it has comparatively little about Jesus' early life, teaching ministry and resurrection appearances; and conversely, in some accounts of Christian origins since the early nineteenth century, it has been seen as the simple and unadorned version of a story that Matthew, Luke and (especially) John then surround with complexities. It is true that Mark's brevity and intensity set it apart; but it is a mistake to think that this means it is naïve and 'primitive'. Mark is shot through with deeply theological perspectives, at least as much as the other Gospels, but the evangelist manages to embody these insights in a whole range of skilful storytelling techniques and turns of phrase. Putting great depth into apparently simple stories is something requiring enormous skill, and Mark is a great artist in this respect.

That is why I describe these reflections as an attempt to help us read Mark slowly, to go back over the surface simplicity of the text and tune in to some of the deeper themes – above all to listen to the various ways in which Mark is challenging us not simply to read but to expose ourselves to a new and transforming relationship with the figure at the heart of his story. The point of the Gospel is that we should encounter there a reality alarmingly beyond human expectation and human capacity; and that through this encounter we should be changed bit by bit into the sort of person who can actually understand what is asked from us and what has been made possible for us in the life and death and rising of Jesus.

I have tried not to take for granted too much knowledge of the biblical text overall, or of the ancient world, and apologize if I have failed to get this right. I have quoted some significant Christian writers who have found that Mark's text leaves them with an unmistakeable sense of a living presence at work in it. And my hope is that readers of these meditations may be prompted to go back to Mark's little book and let it work on them afresh, so that the same living presence may dawn on them as well.

Thanks to Jonathan and Sarah Goodall, as always, for help with the recordings and transcriptions, and to Philip Law of SPCK for further suggestions in tidying up the text; also to all who came to the lectures and asked such searching questions afterwards; and to the Dean and Chapter and choir of Canterbury Cathedral for so generously collaborating with the organizing and presenting of the lectures.

Rowan Williams
Cambridge
Lent 2014

1

The beginning of the Gospel

The Gospel according to St Mark can seem like something of a Cinderella among the Gospels. For many hundreds of years it was used in public worship far less than any other of the Gospels. It never attracted the great – indeed the encyclopaedic – commentaries of scholars and saints across the centuries. Unlike St John's Gospel, where everybody who was anybody in the history of the Christian Church seemed to want to write a commentary on it, St Mark attracted relatively little attention from the great expositors of Scripture in the early and mediaeval Church. Its brevity made it seem less useful than the fuller accounts of the other Gospel writers, and its style and language are apparently very straightforward (apparently; as we shall see, there's rather more to it than that). In the most solemn week of the Christian year, the week leading up to Easter, it was the narratives of Matthew and John that were used in public worship and that eventually attracted the great musical settings like those of Johann Sebastian Bach (he did write a setting of Mark's Passion narrative but nothing survives, probably because it would not have had a prominent place in the regular liturgy of Holy Week like the others).

And yet, Mark's Gospel still has, for all sorts of readers, an exceptional impact. Two of the foremost Christian communicators of the twentieth century – one of them happily still with us – have claimed that they owe their Christian faith simply to reading Mark without any particular preparation. The great German Protestant theologian Jürgen Moltmann was a prisoner of war in Scotland in 1945; he and his fellow-prisoners had just been shown photographs of the horrors in the camps of Belsen and Buchenwald, and were dealing with the nightmare realization that they had been fighting for a regime responsible for unimagined atrocity. Moltmann had little Christian background and no theological education, but when an army chaplain distributed copies of the Bible,

> I read Mark's Gospel as a whole and came to the story of the passion; when I heard Jesus' death cry, 'My God, my God, why have you forsaken me?' I felt growing within me the conviction: this is someone who understands you completely, who is with you in your cry to God and has felt the same forsakenness you are living in now . . . I summoned up the courage to live again.[1]

A similar story is told by the late Metropolitan Anthony Bloom, who did so much to open up to Westerners the

Russian Orthodox tradition of prayer. As a sceptical young man he had been persuaded to attend a camp for young Russians, and attended an address by a celebrated and very saintly Orthodox theologian. The address infuriated and disgusted him, and he went home determined to confirm for himself the emptiness and stupidity of Christianity by reading the Gospels; he chose to start with Mark simply because it was the shortest.

> The feeling I had occurs sometimes when you are walking along in the street, and suddenly you turn round because you feel someone is looking at you. While I was reading, before I reached the beginning of the third chapter, I suddenly became aware that on the other side of my desk there was a Presence . . .
>
> I realized immediately: if Christ is standing here alive, that means he is the risen Christ.[2]

He committed himself there and then to the Christian faith and lived it out in a variety of costly ways for the next seventy years, bringing many other people to the acknowledgement of that same Presence he had encountered.

What is a Gospel?

With such testimonies, it would obviously be rash to ignore a text like this. It is a puzzling book, though; and it would have been puzzling for a reader taking it up in the first

Christian century, perhaps just as puzzling as it is today. We know from the letters of St Paul that – by the time Mark was probably written – the word for 'good news', *euangelion* in Greek, was already commonly used by Christians as a sort of shorthand for the Christian story, the Christian message. A book called 'The Good News about Jesus' would not have been too surprising for a Christian of that era. But if you didn't happen to be an insider and you came across a book with a title like this, what would you think? *Euangelion* is actually a piece of political jargon. *Euangelion*, literally 'a bit of good news' or 'a pleasing message', was the word you would have used in the ancient world as the routine official designation for an important public announcement. An *euangelion* was a press release from the Buckingham Palace or Downing Street of the day announcing a significant event of public interest: the emperor's son had got engaged or had been invested with some dignity, a princess had had a baby, the army had defeated the Germans, a city on the border of the Persian Empire had been captured. Something had happened to be glad about; but, a bit more than that, the something that had happened was likely in some way, great or small, to change things in public life. An *euangelion*, a 'gospel', a good message, is a message about something that alters the climate in which people live, changing the politics and the possibilities; it transforms the landscape of social life.

So if you were a Greek-speaking subject of the Roman Empire, living somewhere around the eastern Mediterranean, that's the set of associations you would have picked up if you'd happened upon this book – apparently the reading material of a small and eccentric and rather worrying religious sect. It is meant to be an official proclamation, and its opening words state that this is the beginning of an official proclamation about someone called 'Jesus the anointed, God's son'. Who is Jesus? What does it mean that he's called 'anointed'? And why exactly is this Jesus given the royal title of a Child of God? The very first verse of Mark's Gospel would tell you that this was a book about 'regime change'; someone's new reign has been inaugurated. And that is of course exactly what Mark reinforces when he summarizes the preaching of Jesus himself. Jesus' first words in the Gospel are an announcement that the kingdom of God is at hand:

> After John had been handed over for imprisonment, Jesus went into Galilee announcing the official proclamation about God. The time has arrived, he said, the rule of God has come close, so change your minds. Trust this proclamation.
>
> (Mark 1.14)

It sounds odd when we strip away some of the familiar vocabulary of our translations, but something like this would have been what people heard when they didn't have two thousand years of Christian reading behind them. It's an announcement that God is taking over. And so the reader is warned from the very first verse of Mark's Gospel that she or he must look and listen in the Gospel for all the things that change the state of affairs in the world. This is going to be a book about change, a book about how the world came to look different, under different management. The title and the first chapter give warning to the reader that this is not just a chronicle about someone in the past; this is about how a particular person's life altered the shape of what was possible for you and me, the readers.

Does this mean that it's not a book of history or biography? A very interesting and rather complicated question. My imaginary reader in the ancient world would have seen it as actually quite like some ancient books of biography. In the ancient world a biography was not one of those 600-page doorstoppers that you pick up in Waterstones, telling you everything you wanted to know, and quite a lot more, about some fleetingly famous politician or celebrity. An ancient biography would build up a series of anecdotes which would give you something like a set of snapshots, pictures of your subject in this situation or that. You would thus have a chance to look at the main figure from several different points of view, in different situations, and you'd build up from that some sense of what kind of person he or she was. Mark's method is not unlike that. He doesn't bother too much about chronology. He doesn't give you any dates. He doesn't give you anything much like a connected story for the greater part of the Gospel, but he gives you these 'snapshots'. Here is the anointed Jesus doing this, doing that, meeting one person, then another, drawing forth this reaction, then that. And as you work through this collection of apparently disconnected anecdotes, you begin to see what sort of person he is – and also perhaps on a second reading to see how the arrangement of the anecdotes is nowhere near as random as might at first appear. In the jargon of the scholars this means that Mark is mostly composed of what scholars call *pericopai* – paragraphs of information leading to a kind of punch line and a report of people's reactions. 'So he said . . . and they were all amazed!' That is how so many stories are told in Mark. It means that it would not have been by any means unrecognizable as history or biography; but there are elements that alert the reader that this is going to be no ordinary biography.

Who was Mark?

At this point, we need to step back a little bit before getting on to the real meat of what the Gospel has to say, and look very briefly at some of the scholarly debates about Mark that have been going on over the last half-century. It isn't a simple story. The more people began to recognize the way Mark was built up – short snappy stories with a punch line – the more they thought that these stories had all the characteristics of traditions that have been passed down from generation to generation and polished carefully in their use by a whole community. This insight depended quite a lot on twentieth-century scholarship that had dealt with the development of folk-tales, showing how their form developed over generations. The problems began to arise when people concluded that in that case the reader could safely ignore any idea that Mark depended on first-hand witness. Mark was just collecting – as you might say – the folk-tales of his community, and exactly what their origin was we couldn't know. What we could know was something about the point they were meant to make in their developed form, polished by the retellings of a community. What their precise link was with anything Jesus said and did was bound to be obscure at best, and not of first importance. What matters for us as contemporary readers is working out the agenda of the writer and the community around him as he interprets the tradition to make sense for his own generation.

There are some problems here about the nature of history and tradition which we'd better put on one side for the moment; but the biggest difficulty with this approach – a difficulty that's been recognized in scholarship for about forty years – is that it makes Mark himself, the writer, a rather dim and shadowy personality. Scholars began to say that it did not make sense after all to see Mark as just stringing together an assortment of anonymous folk-tales. The closer you look, the more obvious it is that Mark is thinking very carefully about how he places his stories: what belongs here, what belongs there. He nudges you constantly with little echoes and allusions, as if to say, 'You remember I said a few pages back . . . ? Bear that in mind, because this ought to click with that.' As I'll try to show in these meditations, there's even a kind of echo between the very beginning and the very end. Mark is not a naïve writer, not somebody who simply has a card-index of useful stories about Jesus that he's heard in Sunday school and is threading them together with no particular plan. He has a creative role as an individual writer. He has a single, connected message to give, an *euangelion*, an announcement, to make; and he is, to that extent, very much in control of his material.

But the whole question of the origins of his material remains a live one. A lot of scholars would now agree that in the mid-twentieth century the pendulum swung much too far in the direction of thinking that the stories here are essentially formed in the common life of the community – not personal reminiscence or personal creation, but formulaic stories emerging and being passed on. The question has been re-opened as to where and how the tradition begins. As we shall see later on, the opposition between individual memory and collective history is not nearly as simple as you might think. Some scholars, including especially Richard Bauckham of St Andrews, have argued recently that we have taught ourselves to be much too suspicious about the origins of traditions in the New Testament and even traditions about the New Testament. The text is written well within the period when personal eyewitness memory would have been alive. If within, say, forty years of the likely writing of Mark's Gospel there is a fairly coherent tradition about how it was written and by whom, we should think twice before just writing it off. And there is indeed such a tradition from very early in the second century – that the Mark who wrote the Gospel was the secretary of St Peter. Early in the second century a bishop in what is now Turkey recorded some of what he had picked up from his sources in the churches of Asia Minor, and one of the traditions he noted was that Mark took down what Peter had said, not putting it down in any particular order, but 'interpreting' what Peter was saying so that it would be accessible to new hearers and readers (there is also a casual and completely random detail that St Mark was known as Mark the 'short-fingered' – whether because he was thought to have this physical characteristic or because he wrote so briefly and economically, we don't know).

Now we know from the New Testament that there was an early tradition that Mark was indeed associated with Peter. In the first letter ascribed to St Peter (1 Peter 5.13), the writer speaks of 'my son Mark' being with him in 'Babylon' – probably Rome. It's often been assumed that this is the same Mark who travelled with Paul, quarrelled with him (like a good many others), and eventually seems to have made it up with him (again, happily, like a good many others). So there you have one way of looking at the beginnings of the Gospel. Peter, preaching around the Mediterranean and particularly in Rome, makes use of a younger associate, a secretary or interpreter who writes down what he says but not in historical or chronological order. It is a tradition that has had quite a sceptical reception in modern scholarship; but some at least, as I've said, have begun to wonder whether we need to be quite so suspicious. I want to note just two initial points which might make us pause before we dismiss it entirely.

The first is, interestingly, that it doesn't make a claim for direct eyewitness testimony. If you wanted to make up a legend about St Mark, you would surely be very tempted to say that he saw it all happen and wrote it down. But instead, it's never presented as other than second-level testimony (contrast St John's Gospel, which repeatedly points us to the testimony of someone who was present at the events recorded, and which was regarded from the earliest times as being directly based on the witness of a disciple): Mark listened to what Peter said, and wrote it down as best he could. And the second point is the recognition from early on that his text is not organized in a clear and tidy chronology. Perhaps the early second-century writers were simply puzzled by the way Mark was organized – as many of us might be; but the interesting thing is that they did not dismiss this brief and superficially hurried text entirely, in favour of the fuller and more systematic narratives of Matthew and Luke: as if there were something that gave Mark a distinctive quality. So it may be premature to write off the tradition of a connection with Peter; whether true or not, it explains why the Gospel found a footing.

Is the Mark in question the Mark we read about in the Acts of the Apostles, who travelled with Paul? The nuisance is that Mark is possibly the commonest name in the Roman Empire; there will have been any number of Marks around in any early Christian community. But to identify the author of a Gospel by a very common name might suggest that people were expected to know which of the countless Marks in the Roman Empire was in question (if somebody were to circulate a text under the title of 'Will's Book', you would expect that the intended readership would have an idea which Will had written it). There is a case, then, for the Gospel being associated with a Mark who was sufficiently high-profile in the early Church for people to recognize him – perhaps a Mark who had been a companion to one or both of the great apostles, the Mark of the Acts of the Apostles and of 1 Peter, of Colossians 4 and 2 Timothy 4.

There is one small cluster of possibly supportive evidence, though it is bound to be speculative. The Mark of the Acts of the Apostles, John Mark, belongs to what is obviously quite a well-to-do family in Jerusalem, a family which, like many such families, apparently has overseas connections, presumably through trading interests. Mark, we are told (Acts 12.25), is close to (perhaps related to) Barnabas, the wealthy merchant from Cyprus who joined the Christian community and made over his property to it. It sounds as though Mark in Jerusalem fits into a network connecting

Judaea with the Jewish trading settlements elsewhere in the Mediterranean – a very common pattern, which in itself doesn't tell us a great deal. Such networks and trading concerns were likely to have several outposts around the eastern Mediterranean; Jerusalem, Cyprus and Cyrene in North Africa were closely in touch (and we hear in Acts 11.20 of Christians from Cyprus and Cyrene leaving Jerusalem to preach in Antioch).

Now the mention of Cyrene might make us prick up our ears in relation to Mark's Gospel; the one passage in the text which claims something close to first-hand testimony occurs in the story of Jesus' trial and death, where we are informed (Mark 15.21) that Jesus' cross was carried by Simon from Cyrene, 'the father of Alexander and Rufus'. There can be no serious doubt that the author of the Gospel expects his audience or readers to know who Alexander and Rufus are; that is, he assumes that they will be familiar with what is almost certainly another eastern Mediterranean Jewish trading family with members and connections in different cities – one of whom, by an extraordinary historical accident, was directly involved in the events of Good Friday. There is no intelligible reason for the preservation of those names, Alexander and Rufus, unless there's a personal connection. A Mark who lived in a community where Alexander and Rufus of Cyrene were familiar figures would fit comfortably with a Mark whose Jerusalem family had connections with the cosmopolitan world of merchants moving around in the

Mediterranean, at home in the great Jewish colonies of North Africa and Cyprus.

So we could conclude that it's not unlikely that the Mark who wrote the Gospel is part of a particular social world, mobile, prosperous, moderately educated (otherwise I doubt whether St Paul would have wanted to make use of his services): a seriously helpful assistant for a wandering apostle. But at the heart of this stand Alexander and Rufus: they represent the point in the Gospel at which – you might say – we are one handshake away from the first Good Friday. Simon of Cyrene, of course, has commonly been portrayed in modern Christian art as an African; and the appropriateness of see-ing the cross of Jesus carried by a man from that oppressed and abused continent has been so overwhelmingly obvious in so many people's eyes that it is hard to challenge it – and the image itself of the cross carried by an African is a right and a crucial one. But we do as historians have to reckon with the fact that Simon of Cyrene has an unmistakeably Jewish name; and the only really plausible reason for some-one from Cyrene being in Jerusalem for a Jewish feast is that he is a Jew from the diaspora trading community who has come on pilgrimage (I was one of those involved in the 1980s in founding the Simon of Cyrene Theological Institute for the theological training of ministerial candidates from minority ethnic backgrounds in this country; my scholarly conscience and my Christian conscience were and are some-what in tension over the use of the name . . .).

All of this also helps to make some sense of another ancient tradition which associates St Mark with Alexandria in Egypt, of which he is the patron. In the traditions of the Egyptian church, this is not only an association with Alexandria, however; it's also, surprisingly at first, with Libya – which is where Cyrene is situated (I have listened in Libya to people repeating venerable Arabic traditions about Mark's time of residence in the east of that country; there is a cave identified as a place where he spent time in solitude). We cannot know how ancient or reliable these traditions are; but a picture comes together which makes rough historical and social sense, the picture of a Gospel writer with quite widely flung links in cities of the Jewish diaspora. But it still leaves open the question of exactly where, let alone when, the Gospel was composed. At various times, scholars have declared with absolute certainty for Rome, Syria, northern Palestine and indeed several other places as well. Rome probably still leads the field; but I confess to being tempted by the case for Jewish–Roman North Africa, with its very close associations both with Jerusalem and with Rome.

Which takes us to Mark's language. The Greek that he writes is not very literary: it's not bad (certainly not like the bizarrely ungrammatical Greek of the Revelation of St John). Mark writes what you might call ordinary *Daily Mail* Greek, of the kind that professionals and travellers in the Mediterranean area would have used, a Greek that has picked up some Latin turns of phrase and even vocabulary. Mark occasionally makes use of Latin words in Greek spelling of just the kind that would have been used in the coastal cities around the Mediterranean. It's the Greek of the big cosmopolitan trading towns, not the Greek of the study or of the literary classes. It is the language of a reasonably educated but not very bookish merchant class, with those tell-tale little Latin words stuck in. Matthew and Luke, in contrast – Luke particularly – like to make sure that they have the right words in Greek. The difference comes across in the words that Mark uses for Roman officials or for the local coinage, for example. And all this is, alas, no help at all in working out where it was written; that has to remain an open question, but the likelihood is clearly one of the commercial centres around the Great Sea.

As for the date: one helpful scholar remarked recently that it was either just after or just before AD 70 – which is not very illuminating for anyone who wants a straight answer. AD 70 was of course for the Jewish people the most traumatic date in the first Christian century, the year when Jerusalem was attacked and captured by the Roman army of Vespasian and Titus, when the independent administration of Judaea disappeared and the Temple was destroyed and the whole country laid waste. So when you read in Mark's Gospel (chapter 13) the prophecies Jesus gives of coming troubles, you have a choice between believing that Jesus foresaw the coming troubles, or believing that Mark is using hindsight to polish, focus and dramatically expand some remembered

his every word precisely in a public meeting, or a whole lot of anonymous traditions washing around in a community and waiting for an editor, or an independent writer crafting semi-fictional stories to illustrate his theology. Anyone who has listened to anecdotes being told in the Middle East today will soon get a glimpse of how the process works; and it is certainly none of the above. When I first visited Egypt, over thirty years ago, and spent time with some of the monks in the desert communities, I realized for the first time what sort of process the first composition of St Mark's Gospel might have been. You would hear people telling stories about a favourite monk from one of the great monasteries: 'One day, Fr Philemon was going to so-and-so. And a man said to him . . . and he said . . . and the man replied . . . and Fr Philemon said . . . and they were amazed. And another time, Fr Philemon was going on a journey and the guard on the train said to Fr Philemon . . .' and so it goes on. Or there is the literature that we have about one of the great Greek saints of the twentieth century, Elder Porphyrios, who died some years ago, and these books are cast in very much the same way. Testimony is gathered from a wide range of people ('I remember when Fr Porphyrios came and spoke to us at such and such a convent . . . and he said . . . and we said . . . and we asked him . . . and he said . . .') and the stories are strung together to make a point or illustrate a theme. The individual testimony and the community process work together: it is certainly not a question of the stories simply being created by communities or by individuals to serve their own purpose – the process is richer and deeper than that. Equally, it is not a question of a strict relating of unchallengeable fact. You could express the point by saying that the narrative crystallizes a relationship. Telling stories like this about Fr Philemon or Elder Porphyrios or Jesus of Nazareth is not telling stories about a distant presence of third-person interest, but witnessing to a relationship that makes a dramatic difference. You, and the way you live, speak and act now, are part of the difference they have made.

The question of whether – to take one of the more dramatic stories I heard in Egypt – Fr Philemon ever did actually stop a train by his prayers is not one that you can answer very straightforwardly (granted that it is quite unusual to stop trains by prayer). But what is it like to encounter, to be in relationship with, a person whom you could very well believe to be capable of stopping a train by prayer? What matters is not trawling through the records of the railway company to get a clear yes or no (which would be unlikely even with comprehensive documentation; who knows exactly why trains break down at this rather than that point?), but trying to understand what is the nature of the relationship that has persuaded you that the world is that different, that surprising, that exciting, that you can just about imagine trains being stopped by prayer. Unless we're prepared to see Mark's Gospel in something of this light, we may misunderstand it and become caught in a standoff between obstinate literalism about every detail and obstinate scepticism about everything that sounds 'supernatural'. That is the way to avoid the real challenge, the difficulty and the promise of the Gospel. The narrative first and foremost depicts and seeks to realize for us, the readers, a relationship within which the stories make sense and are credible: we're not being invited to make a detached judgement. Which is not a roundabout way of saying that the miracles in Mark are not real, but to say that to read the miracle stories in Mark is precisely not to read a series of remarkable magical happenings. It is to read about a person around whom extraordinary things happened, whatever the exact detail, and to see that such storytelling about these events becomes credible because it has changed the teller and the hearer, has created a relationship of utter confidence which is now offered to the reader/listener to share.

So the text of St Mark's Gospel sets out two challenges for the reader. The first is simply to let yourself be addressed by this central figure. The storyteller Mark is writing out of a relationship, a compelling relationship which it is his purpose to make real to you, so that whether or not you want to be in the same kind of relationship, you have to pay attention to the fact of the relation as the writer presents it. And so, second, you have to grasp and share in the changed state of affairs to which the story testifies – the changed state of affairs which is now being officially announced in an *euangelion*, a press release from the palace, which has changed the political climate, which has changed the regime. Those are the challenges: can you allow yourself to be spoken to by this figure? can you therefore enter into the changed state of affairs that his story is about?

Charles Williams, the great Anglican poet, critic and playwright, wrote memorably about Mark that what is said about the kingdom of God in the Gospel is 'not a state of being without which one can get along very well. To lose it is to lose everything else.'[3] This expresses very well the total change of perspective that's being evoked; and he goes on to say that you can't just take out material about the kingdom of God and the coming of judgement from Mark – the material usually referred to as 'apocalyptic' – and expect it to stay the same. 'To remove the apocalyptic is not to leave the ethical but to leave nothing at all.' This is a story, says Williams, in the first chapter of which 'Witness is born out of heaven and on earth and from hell.'[4] It is a superb summary of that first chapter – the voice from heaven at the baptism of Jesus (Mark 1.11); the witness given to Jesus in the response of the people who recognize the exceptional authority and newness of what he says and how he says it (1.27); and the voice of the demons who protest at his presence (1.24, 34). This is – we are being warned – a deeply serious story, a world-changing story, whose ramifications extend well beyond the villages of Palestine. And if these events do indeed change the world – change the regime – then the central figure is someone who has the authority and the capacity to change anything and everything in the world. To quote Charles Williams' great friend, C.S. Lewis, 'He's not a tame lion, you know.' No accident that Mark's traditional symbol in Christian art is a lion.

The point is made as soon as the Gospel begins. Mark brings off a great narrative triumph by pushing Jesus on to the stage without a word of introduction. He doesn't tell you who this is beyond his name and his place of origin – no family background, no Christmas story. The curtain goes up with a clatter, and there on stage is the central figure; no prelude, no apologies, no explanations, there is the anointed one. And that is how the text will go on; which is why the Jesus of St Mark is not – as some unimaginative readers of an earlier generation sometimes thought – an innocent and straightforward human prophet devoid of all the theological trappings that gather around him in the other Gospels. On the contrary: this Jesus is arguably stranger, more 'transcendent', more simply worrying than the Jesus of any of the other Gospels. And now we must go on to investigate just what sort of change he is supposed to have brought about.

2

Telling secrets

W e have begun to think in general terms about what kind of book St Mark's Gospel is, and we have tried to identify the double demand that it makes of its readers: the demand to entertain the relationship into which the writer seeks to draw us, and so to enter into the effects of the great public event of 'regime change' in the world, which is announced solemnly and formally in the very word *euangelion* – gospel.

But we must come to terms with one of the most puzzling and most frequently discussed aspects of the Gospel, a theme which, paradoxically, seems to pull us away from the initial drama of a great public announcement. This is a book all about proclamation, dedicated to announcing something; yet, again and again, the Jesus of St Mark underlines the need for secrecy. When he exorcises evil spirits, 'he did not allow the demons to speak because they knew him' (1.34); when he heals a leper, he says, 'Take care to say nothing to anyone' (1.44). And so it goes on throughout the Gospel. In one famous (or notorious) passage, he goes still further:

after telling the parable of the sower scattering his seed on bad ground and good, he finishes with the defiant 'Anyone who has ears to hear, let them hear' (4.9), and then goes on to spell out for his disciples the paradox of a public teaching that remains secret:

> When he was on his own, the twelve and some others with them asked him about the parables [or possibly: questioned the way he used parables]. And he said, 'To you the secret of the kingdom of God has been given. But for those outside, everything gets treated in parables, so that they may see and see but never understand: so that they may hear and hear but never take it in, in case they change their minds and get forgiven.'   (4.10–12)

It is a baffling remark that continues to puzzle many readers of the Gospel; and if we are going to make any sense of it, we have to think about the broad context and content of the Gospel story. So let us stay for a moment with those repeated instructions to tell no one about what has happened. Several times Jesus performs a miracle and instantly says, 'Don't tell anyone about it' (1.44, 3.12, 7.36, 8.26, for example). Of course, in virtually every case he is disobeyed. But why this emphasis on secrecy? It comes up in a different way in two or three other passages that don't have to do with miracles in quite the same way. When Peter confesses his faith in Jesus as the anointed of God (8.29), Jesus instantly tells him and the other disciples that they are on no account to say a word about it. In the chapter that follows, when Peter, James and John are coming down the mountain after seeing Jesus transfigured in blinding light, the same instructions are given: 'Don't say a word to anyone' (9.9), at least not until 'the Son of Man' has been raised from death. You can see something of the same in an episode much further on in the Gospel, in chapter 11, where the authorities in Jerusalem ask Jesus by what authority he does what he does; and Jesus gives a very teasing and indirect answer. Jesus doesn't want, it seems, to be known as a miracle worker, or to base his authority on working miracles.

Yet he does perform miracles, almost as if he cannot stop himself performing miracles when his compassion is engaged. And this already complex picture is made even more complex by the fact that on two occasions he does seem to be expecting people to witness a miracle and draw conclusions. In chapter 2, we have the vivid story (2.1–12) of a paralysed man let down by his friends through the roof of the house in which Jesus is teaching. Jesus says to him, 'Your sins are forgiven.' Some of the more religiously self-important bystanders say, 'Who could possibly claim to forgive sins?' And Jesus rounds on them and says, in effect, 'Do you think it's easier to forgive sins than to do miracles? Look, here's a miracle – stand on your feet, you're cured. That's easy. The difficult thing is forgiving sins.' So the miracle there becomes, in a strange way, not exactly an afterthought but something quite subsidiary to the main point. Jesus is saying, 'I am here to declare to you liberation from sin; and if you think that this is a matter of empty words easily said, think again.' As the Gospel unfolds, we see precisely why it is not easier to say, 'Your sins are forgiven' than to say, 'Get up and walk.'

On another occasion (5.1–20) when Jesus has healed a demon-possessed man from Gerasa, he specifically tells the healed man to go and share the news of what God has done (19). Here, Jesus is working among people who are not Jews; and it seems as though things can be said in this context that cannot in the context of his own people – as though the possibilities of misunderstanding are less. The only moment when Jesus speaks unambiguously about who he is in the context of his own people and culture is at his trial before the High Priest, when he is asked directly, 'Are you the anointed? Are you the Son of God?' Jesus replies, 'I am.' The secret is unveiled; the silence is ended.

Why miracles?

One of the most important themes in modern scholarly discussion of Mark is the idea of the 'Messianic Secret'. As we have seen, Mark's Jesus never announces himself to be the Messiah, the anointed, until the dramatic moment at his trial. Many scholars have offered what in retrospect seems a rather over-simple account of this, arguing that the 'real', historical Jesus never claimed anything for himself, that an early Church which believed that he was the Messiah had to project backwards into Jesus' life the idea that he deliberately concealed his knowledge of his own vocation from all but a few intimates. The instructions to say nothing are the product of an embarrassment felt by the early believers about the relative lack of any evidence that Jesus declared who he was. But it is hard not to feel that such a reading rather misses the important point. Mark is not trying to overcome an embarrassment about the fact that Jesus didn't have enough to say about himself theologically; he is very clear that Jesus is indeed saying something theologically very revolutionary and very challenging about himself. And that is precisely why he preserves these traditions of Jesus instructing people to keep silence. What Jesus has to say is so open to misinterpretation that it could not have been spoken.

So what exactly is the undertow here in this language about secrets? The first miracle performed by Jesus – the cure of the leper – in chapter 1 of the Gospel contains a very odd phrase for which there are two versions in the ancient manuscripts. The leper comes and says, 'If you want to, you can make me clean.' Jesus, 'stirred with deep compassion', says, 'Of course I want to. You can be clean.' But, according to many early manuscripts, Jesus was 'stirred with deep anger' when he spoke these words. Now whichever of those readings you go for (and there's a good case for either of them), the point is that Jesus is doing a miracle because he is stirred. Whether it is compassion for the suffering of the individual or anger at the grip that disease and prejudice have on the leprous outcast, he is emphatically not performing a miracle to prove a point. And the theme that runs through the Gospel could be summed up in just those terms: Jesus will not do miracles to prove points or win arguments. The story of the healing of the paralysed man does indeed show Jesus in a sense performing a miracle to prove a point; but the point is that the miracle is not the point. The miracle is done so as to divert attention from the healing to the promise of forgiveness, to reinforce the idea that if a miracle is astonishing and difficult, the forgiveness of sins is yet more so.

So when miracles do happen, they arise from that immediacy of compassion or indeed of anger, anger at the way in which sickness imprisons people but also anger at the way in which religious zealotry cannot cope with the promise of release. In the story in chapter 3 about the healing of a man with a withered hand, we are told that Jesus' enemies are watching closely to see if he will perform an act of healing on the Sabbath, and that Jesus feels distress and anger at the distorted vision of human needs and priorities that this shows – anger that the possibility of condemning a controversial teacher is more important than the restoring of someone's ability to earn a living. And Mark also records (6.5) that when Jesus returns to his home town, he is not able to do any significant miracles. He is mocked and rejected by his fellow-townspeople; but he does not respond by winning the argument through miracles. There are, we are told, a few unobtrusive healings, but that is all; no spectacle.

So once again, miracle is being put into perspective. It's being taken for granted that Jesus is indeed a healer and an exorcist and that the miracles he performs are real. But what Jesus himself refuses to do is to base his authority on 'signs and wonders'. The story about the paralysed man is very telling in this respect. It is almost as if Jesus is saying that there are plenty of miracle workers, healers and exorcists; and indeed in the world in which Jesus lived, lots of people there were. Charismatic healers wandered around the ancient Near East in substantial numbers, it seems, and in that sense Jesus was a familiar figure in the Mediterranean scene of his day. It seems that Jesus is discouraging his audience from treating him in this familiar and simple category – another charismatic healer – and challenging them to recognize what is unique in his mission.

And that is something a good deal deeper than miracle. Jesus will perform miracles out of compassion – out of an awareness of human solidarity, we could say; but the other side of this is that he will require trust or belief from those with whom he works (as in 9.21–24). Trust heals people (10.52); or, to connect this with our first chapter, we could say that Jesus' healings are always bound into a relation between him and the person to be healed. In the story about his visit to his home town, the reason he can't do mighty works there is, it's implied, that people don't trust him. They remember him as a local labourer, they know his family: the relation is one of casual familiarity and a bit of contempt or snobbery; they cannot trust him to be different, to be himself. But as we have seen, it's made very clear in several of the healing stories that miracles of healing require a relationship, require someone to put his or her trust in Jesus. He will ask, 'Do you believe I can do this?' He will ask, 'What do you really want me to do?' And out of that meeting of trust and compassion comes the miracle.

Mark is a Gospel about relationship. It makes no sense outside the relationship that the writer and the potential reader may have to its central figure. And of course you cannot have a relationship with sheer arbitrary power. A saviour who walks through Galilee and Judaea healing and doing wonders 'at random' would not be somebody who invited relationship. Such a saviour might invite wonder, awe, admiration or bafflement – but not necessarily trust. Mark is treading a delicate line here, with much subtlety: he wants us to start from the two basic insights that it is not miracle that is the unique or special thing about Jesus, and that miracle itself, when it occurs, involves trust and relationship. It is never a kind of magic, a display of power and control.

When Jesus is pressed to perform miracles precisely to prove a point, he reacts very sharply and negatively. We might look again at that story in chapter 9, quite a challenging one. Jesus and the disciples have come down from the mountain where he has been transfigured; and at the foot of the mountain they see a large crowd around the other disciples. There is a fierce argument going on, with the 'teachers of the law' disputing with the disciples.

> At once the whole crowd was struck with astonishment when they saw him. They ran to him to greet him, and he asked them, 'What are you arguing with them about?' And a man from the crowd answered, 'Teacher, I brought my son to you – he has a spirit in him that stops him speaking . . . I asked your disciples to throw out the spirit, but they were not able to.' Jesus said in reply, 'Oh, this is a suspicious lot of people! How long do I have to stay with you? How long do I have to put up with you? Now: bring the boy to me.'
>
> (9.14–19)

It sounds quite harsh, as if Jesus is saying, 'Must I really perform a miracle? Won't you leave me alone?' But it transpires, as the conversation goes on, that what Jesus wants to know is whether the boy's father trusts him, and whether he and the others around are simply looking for a miracle to clinch an argument; we are told, notice, that the disciples and the teachers and the crowd had been arguing. So that Jesus' first reaction is, 'Do you – disciples, crowd, even father – want me to do a miracle to win an argument for you?' The boy falls down in convulsions (not hard to imagine; the scene must have been frightening, noisy and disturbing); and in an astonishingly intimate moment with the boy's father – both Jesus and the father, we can imagine, on their knees beside the boy on the ground – Jesus probes gently about the history of the condition: 'How long has this been going on?' The father says, 'Since he was small,' and goes on to describe the life-threatening nature of what happens. Then he appeals directly, 'If you can do something, do it.' And Jesus replies, 'If you can do something . . . ? Well, anything is possible if you trust.' The boy's father responds at once, 'I trust you! Just help me cope where trust falls short.' Or, in the more familiar King James translation, 'Lord, I believe. Help thou mine unbelief.' We need to read the story as one about Jesus 'quarrying' both for a sense of the real seriousness of the suffering being talked about and for a relationship of trust; he goes behind the arguments, asking directly, 'What is this about?' and 'Do you trust?' and the answer is given. The apparent harshness cannot be denied, but what it opens up is the focal and central theme we have been tracing in the Gospel: a miracle is not an argument-stopper; for healings and exorcisms to be more than super-ficial occasions for wonder, a relationship is needed. And you can't have a relationship with magical powers operating in a vacuum.

So perhaps we are beginning to get a little sense of what the real secret is in this Gospel. The secret is that the event which will change everything, which will bring in the regime of

God, which will forgive sins and release people from guilt and fear, is not an event brought about by naked power. The God who is going to change everything, change for ever the conditions in which human beings live, is a God who is 'beyond' power as we would like to understand it; a God who does not coerce belief or clinch arguments, but who repeatedly demands relation and trust. This is the secret that Mark's Jesus wants to disclose – and it is, in the nature of the case, formidably difficult to disclose. Jesus is indeed a healer, and therefore he heals people; there are circumstances where, in the force of his compassion and indignation at suffering, he cannot stop himself healing people. He may not do miracles to prove a point; but he won't refuse his compassion to an individual to prove a point, either. When he's kneeling on the ground beside the father of the epileptic child, he doesn't say, 'I'm sorry, I can't do anything, because if I heal your child it could be misunderstood' and walk away. He is constantly risking misunderstanding. And this repeated insistence on secrecy – 'Don't go talking about this' – is, it seems, Jesus' way of saying, 'I know I do miracles, and it doesn't matter. How often do I have to tell you? It doesn't matter.'

There is a story told about a deeply saintly priest some seventy years ago who was confessor to an Anglican convent for many years. One of the sisters had been to him for spiritual direction, and they were kneeling together in the chapel afterwards. The sister looked up and thought she saw an angel standing beside the altar; she dug the priest in the ribs and said, 'Look, Father, there's an angel!' The priest very properly said, 'Nonsense, Sister. Get on with your prayers.' The sister closed her eyes and obeyed. Some time later, when she saw the priest again, she rather timidly said, 'I'm sorry, Father, but there really was an angel there, you know'; and he said, 'Of course there was. Saw it myself. So what?' A robustly Marcan attitude to miracles, the same approach that you'll find eloquently set out at great length in Book II of the treatise by St John of the Cross, the sixteenth-century Spanish mystic, called *The Ascent of Mount Carmel*, where he devotes several chapters to discussing strange and apparently miraculous events which may occur in the course of prayer, only to say, in effect, that miracles just happen, for reasons only fully known to God. Don't make much of them; don't expect them; don't refuse them; they just happen.

Why parables?

What, then, are we to make of the passage with which we began this chapter, that strange passage where the disciples ask why Jesus has to talk in parables, and Jesus virtually says, 'I talk in parables so that people won't understand.' Is that Jesus saying, 'I'm deliberately making it difficult so that not everybody can get the point'? Hardly. We need to look harder at what the parables themselves are saying to understand this a little better. Jesus has been delivering a whole sequence of parables in this chapter, and they remind us of what exactly the word 'parable' means in Greek. Originally, *parabole* is simply a comparison; and in fact if you look at the parables in chapter 4, that's what you'll see – comparisons. The kingdom is like this, like that. And here Jesus speaks of the work of God in terms of natural processes – the growth of a seed, the radiating of a lamp or candle when it's lit; as if he's saying that to understand how God works there are any number of clues in the world around you. How does God characteristically work? Not with thunderclaps; not with immensely dramatic and instant-aneous interventions – the sky opening and voices being heard (this may happen at Jesus' baptism, but it isn't a clue as to how God *characteristically* acts in the world). How does God work? Subtly, slowly, from the very depth of being. Or steadily, irresistibly, like the light reaching the corners of the room. He works outwards from the heart of being into the life of every day – not inwards from some distant heaven. This is how God works, and you ought to be able to see it around you in the world God has created and rules.

Comparisons, parables, are Jesus' way of saying to the people listening: you know more than you realize about God; but the trouble is that you look and look, and you don't see, you listen and listen and you don't understand. But there it is, could you but grasp it. There is an interesting echo of this in the so-called Gospel of Thomas (a collection

41

of sayings attributed to Jesus, probably compiled in the second Christian century, though some scholars would like to place it earlier). This text contains a lot of very puzzling and eccentric material, but several sayings either reproduce the words or come close to the spirit of Mark 4 – one in particular. 'Jesus said . . . "The Kingdom of the Father is spread upon the earth, and men do not see it." '[5]

So I suspect that those words in chapter 4 of Mark are an instance – not the only one – of Jesus speaking ironically. 'Why do I use comparisons? Because it seems that however hard people look at the world, they don't get inside the meaning of it. Why do I use parables? So that they won't understand! Why do you think?' It is an irony which reinforces the idea that the biggest problem human beings have when confronted with the truth is that they don't know that they don't know. In St John's Gospel, we find the same theme even more starkly expressed: those who think they can see are in fact the ones who actually have their eyes screwed shut (John 9.39–41). So too in Mark: the people who are really in trouble are those who don't know that their eyes are closed. As in the case of what Jesus says and does about miracles and their meaning, the same point is being made: how exactly does God work to change the world? We all have fantasies of how God ought to work to change the world. The voice from heaven, the mighty demonstration of power, the argument-clincher, the word or act that finally settles everything and takes away any doubt so that nothing more needs to be said . . . Yet God appears oblivious to this.

The literary critic Terry Eagleton, whose recent books on religion have brought a breath of fresh air to some of the public debates between believers and unbelievers, has observed that there are some people (inside and outside the Christian faith) who imagine that if one day a large banner unfurled from heaven with the words 'I'm up here, you idiots!' written on it, that would finally resolve the question of God's existence. But of course, that's not how God works – and it has little to do with what he seems to want. He does not worry about demonstrating his existence to us; our problem is not that we do not know, but that we cannot love. He habitually works – so to speak – 'outwards' from the heart of being, steadily expanding the scope of his action through the actions of the beings he has created. So that Jesus is beginning to suggest to his disciples the daring idea that the way God changes things will be from the heart of the human world, not by intervention from the sky. God is transforming the world, healing its wounds and forgiving and overcoming our failures, by being with and in the processes of the world – above all, in that unique process that is a human life: the life first of Jesus, but then the lives of those who have been called and commissioned by Jesus to be – like him and because of him – places where the work of God can start to blossom and expand in the world.

Why misunderstandings?

There are one or two other things to be said about this theme of secrecy and misunderstanding in the Gospels, and one very important theme has to do with the role of the disciples in the story. It's many times been remarked that the disciples in St Mark are conspicuously stupid. They repeatedly miss the point; they repeatedly have to have things explained in words of one syllable; and there have been some scholars who have suggested that St Mark is deliberately trying to undermine the authority of those who consider themselves successors of the twelve apostles. But I think that this misses the point: because it is absolutely vital to Mark's story that what Jesus says is hard to digest and to understand even by those closest to him. Even those who have most reason for understanding what he's saying are going to get it wrong: and that, of course, is a reassurance to the reader. Mark is saying, 'If you're finding this difficult or shocking, don't be surprised; those who were closest to Jesus found it difficult and shocking too. If you feel stupid and at a loss when confronted with the words and work of Jesus, don't be surprised. You're not the first and you won't be the last.' So the dimness of the apostles is not a point of polemic, an axe being ground: it's basic to the scheme. Jesus in Mark's Gospel appears as someone wrestling with the difficulty of communicating to the disciples things that there are no proper words for – communicating that they have to think again about how God works, and to prepare themselves for greater and greater shocks in understanding this.

I'm tempted to think that perhaps one reason why Mark's Gospel has in it very little teaching of the sort we find in Matthew or Luke is that Mark not only wants to draw our attention away from miracles, he even wants to draw our attention away from conventional teaching. He wants to tell a story and present situations that bring us up short. He doesn't want us to go away discussing the interesting ideas that Jesus has or the poignant stories he tells. He wants you to focus on the person of Jesus and on the relation you might have with him, knowing that only so does the radical change come about. You could almost say that Mark prefers to show us a Jesus who is struggling for words, rather than a Jesus who is a fluent teacher and brilliant storyteller, as in the other Gospels. More than once in the Gospel, we hear Jesus saying something like, 'How do I make this clear to you? What can I say to you? Don't you understand yet?' This is a Jesus who is searching for ways to communicate truths for which there are no clear and simple words.

So it makes some sense that this is a Gospel full of secrets, silences and even misunderstandings, a Gospel which on every page carries a very strongly worded health warning to the reader: don't think you've got it yet! That is what Mark wants his readers to understand. It's just a little bit like the way Buddhists talk about the use of the koan in meditation: you are given a saying or a little story which you're supposed to meditate on until you realize you can't understand it in your ordinary categories, at which point enlightenment breaks in. Mark is a long koan. It's meant to bring us to the edge, to tell us that our understanding will not manage this in clear tidy ways. It's a truth that can't easily be spoken – or rather, as soon as it's spoken it provokes more questioning. We can absorb such a truth only by letting go of what we thought about God and ourselves.

Commentators on Mark have quite often said that you must imagine the Gospel aimed at a Church that is perhaps a bit too much in love with wonderworking and success, a Church that puts too much store by tangible signs of God's favour and God's assistance; and I think there's a great deal in that. But this has to be filled out further by what some other commentators have suggested – that Mark is writing for a Church baffled and fearful because the signs and the miracles aren't coming thick and fast. What is coming thick and fast is persecution and a sense of threat and failure. Mark is writing into the life of communities experiencing fear and disorientation.

It's worth imagining yourself for a moment in that kind of situation – and there is no shortage of parallel situations today in our world. A Christian reading Mark in Afghanistan or northern Nigeria, or parts of rural India or Indonesia, a Christian reading Mark in the old Soviet Union, will read with a depth of understanding that is hard for some of the rest of us, because he or she is living in a setting where God is not stepping down from heaven to solve problems, where suffering and insecurity and even the risk of death are daily facts. These are the sorts of people for whom Mark was writing: writing to reinforce a faith in the God who does not step down from heaven to solve problems but who is already in the heart of the world, holding the suffering and the pain in himself and transforming it by the sheer indestructible energy of his mercy.

Inexorably, we are led towards the story of the Passion, the arrest and trial and execution of Jesus. All these themes about how God does and doesn't work, the emphasis on pushing back against expectations of a God who works miracles to win arguments, all of this is directing us towards the final episode of the Gospel, which we shall be thinking about in the last chapter of this book. But before we turn to that, I want to leap forward to the end of Mark's Gospel, which gives a final twist to some of the themes we have been exploring in this chapter. How does Mark's Gospel finish? The oldest manuscripts finish abruptly at verse 8 of chapter 16. Some of the women who have remained loyal to Jesus make their way to the tomb in the hope of anointing his body for proper burial (because, presumably, his burial on the day of his execution has been hurried and a bit make-shift); they hear a young man in radiant clothes at the tomb telling them that Jesus is not there but has been raised from death and they are instructed to go and share this news with the rest of Jesus' friends. Off they go 'and they said nothing to anybody. They were afraid, you see . . .' And that is where the oldest texts finish; as abruptly as that. I translate it as 'They were afraid, you see . . .' to convey something of the sense the reader should have of the story breaking off in mid-narrative. The Greek (*ephoboounto gar*) has that effect: no other work of literature in Greek ends with that little word *gar* which I've translated 'you see'. It's unexpected and abrupt and leaves us in mid-air. What you will see in your Bibles is in fact the attempt of later writers to tidy this up, adding a quick summary of some of the stories from the other Gospels about the rising of Jesus from the dead. And while I've no doubt that those additions are inspired Scripture just as much as Mark's Gospel is, they're not quite what Mark meant us to read. It sounds as if he wanted us to finish in mid-air.

But here is the supremely ironic point. All through the Gospel Jesus has been telling people not to say things and they do. At the very end people are told to say something, and they don't. Look at the wording in the Greek and you'll find some very close echoes, the same vocabulary. Jesus says to the leper in chapter 1, 'Don't say anything to anyone'; and at the very end, the women 'didn't say anything to anyone'. We are surely meant to pick up the paradox here. At last, the message is clear: here, in the crucified Jesus, is the event in which God has changed the world, the event that is the essential subject matter of the *euangelion*, the official announcement; and nobody wants to talk about it. It's too much of a shock, it's too difficult. The women go back to Jerusalem, unable to find the words to share this mystery with the apostles. Once it was a matter of how easy it would have been to tell the story of Jesus the great healer and wonderworker; all the words were there, ready-made – which is why Jesus tells the witnesses not to use them. Now something has been made clear that has no ready-made words: God has acted in the pain and failure of Jesus and in his torture and execution. Just how are we to talk about that?

Now of course we can say that the women at the tomb must have found the words sooner or later, or there wouldn't be a story at all; the other Gospels offer an assortment of versions. But what Mark wants us to remember is that at the particular moment when it seems that the revelation has finally arrived, when the secret has finally been broken open, people don't know what to do with it. The great event officially announced at the beginning of the Gospel, the regime change the *euangelion* loudly proclaimed, is not a conventional triumph, an episode in the glorious career of a monarch, but a public execution. That is the secret, the mystery. Jesus has spoken (4.11) about 'the secret of the kingdom of God' and warned that it will not be straightforward to talk about and perhaps can only be approached through enigmatic stories and images that demand that we make a response of imagination and trust. We shouldn't then be surprised by the way the Gospel ends. No wonder if it's difficult to find the words: the whole thrust of the story so far has been 'don't think too quickly that you've got the measure of this'.

At the end of his Gospel, Mark is telling us to go back and start again: read the whole story again to see how it has been preparing you for the shock of these last episodes, for the moment of stupefied terror and unimagined renewal at the empty tomb. Don't draw conclusions from Jesus' miracles or teaching; wait to see the great event taking shape as a whole, the event whose centre is the cross. And if you think that sharing this mystery is going to be simple, think again: wait for the last trauma, the miracle of miracles, the resurrection which silences even its most immediate witnesses.

A Gospel of silences, of misunderstandings, of indirect and teasing communication: but this is not for the sake of making things difficult in an arbitrary or unkind way. It is to remind us that if it's the true God who is speaking and being spoken about in this book, this God is not a hugely inflated version of how we would run the universe if we had the chance. He is the God at the ground of everything, who works outwards from the heart of being – not that the change is any less radical or real because of that. Mark's deep scepticism about relying too much on miracles, his careful coolness about including too much teaching that might distract us into having interesting discussions about Jesus' interesting ideas, shows us a Jesus who not only brings about 'regime change' in the world in which we live, but a Jesus who changes for ever what we can say about God.

3

A lifelong passion

About one-third of St Mark's Gospel is taken up with the events of the last week of Jesus' life, the story of Jesus' betrayal, suffering and death, his 'Passion'. It's a very striking proportion, which has led some scholars to describe St Mark as a Passion narrative with a long introduction (by way of comparison, only about one-seventh of the Gospels of Matthew and Luke are taken up with the narrative of Jesus' last days before the crucifixion). And in Mark it's made very clear that, as we move into this section, we're moving into a slightly different atmosphere. A narrative which up to this point has felt quite rushed and packed, even a bit scattergun in its effect, noticeably slows down. There are far more quotations from the Old Testament; and, intriguingly, far more references to specific places in and around Jerusalem. There is careful reference to the time of day when things happened.

What makes this interesting is that many readers have observed how slapdash Mark's geography can appear in the rest of the Gospel. He seems, for example, to be confused as to whether Tyre is north or south of Sidon – though, as one recent commentator remarked, if we were asked unprepared whether Manchester was north or south of Liverpool, a lot of us might have similar problems ... But in contrast to this general aspect of his narrative, there's no doubt at all that when Mark turns to this final period, he has a very specific set of locations in mind. If you read the last couple of chapters carefully, you'll notice that they divide clearly into episodes at particular places: the upstairs room where the Last Supper takes place; the garden on the Mount of Olives; the High Priest's house; the Roman governor's residence; the path to Golgotha, 'the place of the skull', where the executions are performed; and the tomb. And this has suggested to some readers a theory which has a good deal of persuasive force, to the effect that the kernel of this narrative began as a kind of liturgy in Jerusalem[6] – something a little like the Stations of the Cross in the later Church. That's to say, these are texts distilled from the experience of early Christians walking reflectively in the footsteps of Jesus in his own city. At each geographical point in the city, each 'station', at specific times of day, there would be a narrative with some Old Testament quotations to show that these events had been foreseen in the divine plan, and then perhaps some prayers, concluding at the tomb with the announcement that 'He is not here, he is risen.'

This makes very good sense of the way in which the story is told; and it gives a very firm basis to the idea that Mark, along with Matthew and Luke, and John too for that matter, is here depending not just on the narratives passed down from the earliest community, but on a practice of prayer and devotion as well, involving readings and stories constructed for these particular stages of a pilgrimage in the city of Jerusalem. Those of you who know the Old City of Jerusalem today will know that these sites are quite close together; you can indeed walk around them prayerfully inside of a morning. So it may be that when we read the final chapters of Mark's Gospel, we are sharing a little of the worship of the very first communities in the Holy City. This means that the story will already certainly have been structured with care, possibly compressing events into a tighter time frame than was actually the case historically; but it reflects a genuine and early form of prayerful commemoration, the three-hourly intervals between major episodes between nightfall on one day and the next reflecting the Jewish hours of prayer. 'Is it a coincidence', asks one scholar, 'that the least edited of the canonical Passion narratives, Mark 14—16, should provide the most complete form of that strange schedule?'[7]

Jesus alone

One of the governing themes of the way Mark tells the story of these last days is that he constructs a pattern in which Jesus is left more and more visibly alone, repudiated by more and more persons and groups. The disciples run away from him, Peter denies that he knows him, the High Priestly council condemns him, the Roman governor and the soldiers reject and abuse him, and he ends on the cross crying out that God too has abandoned him. The last recorded words of Jesus in the Gospel of Mark are, 'My God, why have you abandoned me?' The intensity of that progression in the last pages of Mark is of great significance in understanding the direction and logic of the entire Gospel. Our attention is focused mercilessly on this one figure: as he is progressively set apart from group after group, authority after authority, friend after friend, it becomes clearer and clearer that he alone has to carry the whole meaning, the whole theological and spiritual weight of what is going on. Nobody provides him with a framework for this, no one has written a script for him to perform. He is alone; when he prays in the Garden of Gethsemane, there is no reply from heaven – so that it is not even that he has a 'set of instructions' from God the Father to shape his response. God is no longer separate from him. He must, through what he does and suffers, establish what the voice of God and the presence of God might mean in this world. We spoke about a God who works outward from the heart of reality: God is now in this part of Mark's story working outwards from the heart of the human Jesus. There is no intervention from a distant heaven. It is a point that some of the other biblical narratives bring out rather more explicitly. So, for example, in Matthew's version (26.53) Jesus says, 'Don't you think God could send twelve legions of angels to help if he wanted to?' But this is not at all how Mark works. His is a more chilling and strange text – chilling and strange because you see it in brief, brightly lit episodes with not very much rationale for what exactly happens at each stage. The legal processes are fantastically arbitrary: the midnight trial before the High Priest and his advisers represents something that Jewish law would have condemned outright. It is a nightmare in which people make senseless accusations that go unsubstantiated; and yet Jesus is condemned. Likewise in the exchanges with the Roman governor, the bizarre incident of Pilate offering to release Jesus or the criminal Barabbas and the crowd's choice of Barabbas: we cannot know what lies behind this, but for a Roman governor to release prisoners in this way is unparalleled.

It may help to think that what this narrative does is to help us see events strictly from the perspective of the victim. When the victims of totalitarian violence and tyranny in our own age tell their stories, as many have, they sound very much like this. Victims typically don't really know what's happening; no one explains, no one justifies what is going on, and they only know that everything is stacked against them and that they have no hope of getting out of this nightmare alive. It's the world captured so memorably in the fiction of Franz Kafka as well as the records of those who have been caught up in the arbitrary terror of political oppression. Perhaps we understand Mark a little bit better if we recognize the echoes of Kafka's account of what it is like to be locked into the workings of a meaningless, non-sensical, but completely irresistible system of power, devoted to your destruction. And this seeing the story from the victim's point of view is deeply significant for the whole of Mark's theology.

Contrast all this with the way St John tells the story of the Passion. Here we have intense debate, Jesus responding either with eloquence or with silence to the diverse challenges flung at him. We have the unforgettable account of Jesus' argument with Pilate, with its great climax in Pilate's question, 'What is truth?' – surely one of the most moving and powerful passages in the whole of Scripture. We are given a sense of the inner dividedness of Pilate, and of how his weakness is contrasted with the implacable silence of his victim who is the one truly in command of events. It is as valid and real a perspective on Jesus' trial and death as Mark's, but the two voices work in radically diverse ways. Mark has none of the sustained drama of John, none of the subtly developed irony that is maintained throughout the whole story; he wants us to see here only the isolation and the sense of arbitrary power closing in. But it is in the middle of all this that Jesus makes his one utterly unambiguous claim. When the High Priest asks (14.61), 'Are you the Anointed One, the Son of the Blessed?' Jesus replies, 'I am.' The placing of this claim, this breaking of the silence, is all-important. It is when Jesus is stripped of all hope, of all power, when he stands alone in the middle of this meaningless nightmare, with no hope of life, it is then and only then that he declares who he is. And he does so in words that evoke the Divine Name itself. God calls himself I AM when he speaks to Moses in the Hebrew Scriptures (Exodus 3.13). Again, there are parallels and contrasts with the way St John tells his story: John has Jesus say, 'I am,' at various crucial stages of the narrative (as in 18.5, when the soldiers come to arrest him), and Mark is no less careful in placing the words. But where John scatters the 'I am' sayings throughout his Gospel, Mark – as always, much more stark and economical – narrows it down to the one moment when you can be under no illusion about what faces Jesus. Then and then only does God declare himself.

'I am,' says Jesus, 'and you will see the Son of Man seated on the right hand of the Power, advancing on the clouds of heaven.' That little phrase, 'Son of Man', has caused endless scholarly discussion, and its full meaning is still obscure; but at the very least, here as in several other places in Mark, it seems to mean 'this mortal being', 'this person here'. 'I am,' says Jesus; and you will see this mortal person, the one who at this moment is alone and facing condemnation to death, seated on God's throne, ready to pass judgement on the world. Think back to our discussion of the secrecy theme in Mark: there can be no words yet for this new revelation of God, a God whose authority appears only when all worldly and human accompaniments of power and success are stripped away, so it is bound to be a secret, a secret that can only be spoken when Jesus himself breaks his silence. The whole Gospel is moving inexorably to this point at his trial before the High Priest.

Mark has set aside the idea that we should listen to Jesus because he does wonderful things, even that we should listen to Jesus because he says wonderful things. If we are to listen to what Jesus is saying in his very existence, his mortal flesh, his death, it is something that can happen only when every possibility of hope, of love, of absolution, has apparently been swept away and all that is left is this bare claim. This mortal person (says Jesus) stands here in the place of God; and the place of God is the place of a rejected and condemned human being. Before Jesus is arrested and condemned, you might still nurture the illusion as you read that it will somehow turn out well. Perhaps there is a future in which Jesus will find support, belief, perhaps after all we shall be able to find words for him in our usual language and vocabulary. But Mark makes quite sure that we cannot sustain any such illusion by this point. This is the 'gospel' moment, the moment of regime change, the event that is to be announced. This is where the world, with all the language we use in and about it, is turned on its head. But – and this is where the news is unimaginably good as well as unimaginably dark and shocking – the new world which is brought into being in this way, the new world which the *euangelion* announces, must be one in which God cannot be dethroned by any degree of pain, disaster or failure. If the helpless, isolated

Jesus declares, 'This mortal man is now where God is,' then God's presence and resource, his love and mercy, cannot be extinguished by loneliness or injustice, by the terrible, apparently meaningless, suffering in which human beings live. God has chosen to be, and to be manifest, at that lowest, weakest point of human experience. And so the poor and the helpless, the condemned and the isolated, reading this story told from the victim's point of view, can know that God is with them, and that the God who is with them cannot be defeated or deposed from his Godhead.

'A lifelong passion' – because, connecting this with the theme of the last chapter, it is possible to see how everything we've read so far in Mark's Gospel does indeed serve as an introduction to this world-changing insight: God is not where you thought he was; God is in and with this mortal man, who is helpless and about to suffer a terrible death. This is where God chooses to be and to declare himself; and the Gospel is the echo of that divine self-declaration.

Human and divine power

If we turn back a few chapters from the trial story, we shall find a hint of this, in the celebrated passage in chapter 10 (35–45) about how the disciples argue about who will be the greatest in the kingdom. Immediately after Jesus has predicted his death, James and John, the sons of Zebedee, come to him asking for a special favour: they want to sit on

Jesus' right and left in his kingdom. They are silenced by Jesus, and the other disciples are angry that James and John have been seeking unfair advantages – and Jesus rounds on them as well, as if to say, 'If you'd had enough courage, you'd probably have asked me for the same favour!' But, he goes on, the whole framework of seeking advantage is exactly what I am here to overturn.

> Those who are highly regarded among the nations lord it over them, officials flex the muscles of their authority, but that is not how it shall be with you. Any one among you who wants to be great must be your slave. If you want to be the first of all, you must be the slave of all. For this mortal person did not come to have slaves attending on him: he came to be a slave. He came to give his life as the price that bought back multitudes.

That key passage (42–45) has been the foundation of generations of speculation about how the redemption of the world is achieved – about the meaning of the 'atonement', the reconciliation between God and humanity that is brought about in the death of Jesus. But the context is not essentially about theories of how the death of Jesus works. Jesus is saying simply that his execution is the price that is paid to free us once and for all from the fantasy that God's power is just like ours, only in a hugely inflated version – as we noted earlier, a matter of what we would do if we were lucky enough to be running the universe. The death of Jesus is the price paid to abolish and uproot that fantasy. It does not only destroy the fantasy that God's power is like ours; it also uproots the corresponding notion that whatever power we attain must be valued and clung to at all costs because it is power endorsed by God. In these lethal errors lie the roots of all our sin and self-inflicted misery, the roots of death. From these errors and their consequences the death of Christ delivers us, dismantling the myth of power that holds us prisoner. In this sense, his life is 'paid over' so that we may be set free, like a ransom paid to a kidnapper.

It is not a carefully phrased theory but a powerful metaphor to conclude an intense argument about the character of God's act and power, Mark's favourite theme. But as soon as people began to look through a microscope at this text the difficulties began to arise. Who is the ransom paid to? Does God have to negotiate with someone else in order to get the human race back? Does the devil have rights over us that God has to observe when he redeems us? And centuries of theological complexity and – to be frank – theological muddle flow from this. Neither Mark nor Mark's Jesus is interested at this point in the story in theories of the atonement. We are being told simply that Jesus uses the language of paying his life over to set us free precisely in the context of saying that what we have to be delivered from is a cruel and imprisoning fantasy about God's power and ours. Let go of all of that and then there is freedom.

And what allows us to let go is what is laid bare in the trial and death of Jesus; that is the difference made by the crucified God, by the God who declares himself in a moment of isolation and helplessness, whose forsakenness speaks – as Jürgen Moltmann discovered so dramatically in his prison camp – to all who have found themselves without anchor or orientation in a world of betrayal and terror.

As we saw when we discussed the miracles, this is anything but an easy message to digest. We have noted already how even the very ending of the Gospel does not give us a simple message, but something more like a problem to solve practically, to solve in action and response: go back and start reading again, because there is no ending to the process of discovering what it is to be turned around and renewed through trust in the risen Jesus. Hardly have you put the Gospel down – Mark implies – than you find some of those fantasies about power beginning to creep back in again. So go back and start again. The story is not finished, the book does not end, so long as we need to be converted afresh.

The event of Jesus' death has indeed, once and for all, exploded the myths; and yet, mysteriously, we behave as if we could still reinstate the terrible error that God's power and ours are the same kind of thing. We reinvent this day after day; so our conversion must happen day after day. The very first witnesses to the resurrection are terrified and they can't find words in which to communicate what they've seen, because what they have seen is God setting his seal on the crucified Jesus, declaring himself in the dead, failed and abandoned Jesus. In the mysterious event of the empty tomb, God says, 'That was not the end; I am alive in Jesus.' And to hear that for the first time, says St Mark, was not a bland bit of religious uplift, but something frightening. So, he says to his readers, don't be at all dismayed if at first or fifth or thirty-fifth reading you find it terrible and frightening too.

But – as again we have already noted – there is, hidden in this, an extra teasing paradox. The women clearly did say something because this Gospel has been written. It did turn out to be possible to find words for what they thought they would never be able to talk about. So if you, the reader, are baffled, dismayed and silenced by the mystery of the cross and the resurrection, don't despair. Words were found, lives have been lived in faith: that's why this book is here, St Mark says, because somebody found it possible to talk about this. And so might you, reader. But the 'somebody' who found it possible to talk about it also reminds us relentlessly just how difficult it is.

The end of the Gospel

The mysterious – do we say miraculous? – ending of Mark throws the ball firmly into our court. And, yet again, we're drawn back to the centrality of the theme of relationship in Mark. The resurrection isn't just something you can point to, as if we could say, 'There is Jesus, walking out of his tomb and showing the High Priest and Pilate and everyone else how wrong they were.' It's the re-creating of a relationship of trust and love on the far side of the most extreme human realities, suffering, abandonment, death. That is what the resurrection story points us to. And so the conclusion of the Gospel is to say to us that faith in the crucified and risen Jesus is possible, and that we must go on reading and listening until we find it, reading and listening until we grasp what it is that Jesus has dismantled and done away with. Some have lived their way into this and found words to carry the reality of that relationship – and here in the Gospel text is the proof that such relationship can happen and that there are such words to be found if you will be patient and brave enough to wait for them.

There are those who have thought that the end of the Gospel is either an accident or – rather like the Messianic Secret – a kind of stratagem. Some have argued that the stories of the risen Jesus must have been created in the generations following the first Easter – and that this increasingly generated a problem as to why there was no early witness to the empty tomb. Mark proposes that no one spoke about the empty tomb because they were told not to. But this is to isolate the empty tomb narrative from the rest of the Gospel and to fail to see how closely it fits with themes that are there from the start. It is to ignore that central and dramatic irony of how the one order to speak of a miracle is initially disregarded – because this miracle, the vindication of the crucified Jesus as bearer of divine authority, is so difficult and revolutionary.

What is to my mind most persuasive about the empty tomb story is the oddity, the unexpectedness of it. And here, as in all the other Gospels, it is worth remembering that, while the rest of the Gospel, especially the Passion story, uses allusions and prophecies from Jewish Scripture to make sense of what's going on, the stories of the resurrection are told with no such allusions. Luke's story of the encounter on the road to Emmaus does indeed refer to the death and rising of Jesus as being foreshadowed in the Scriptures, but doesn't give any specific details. There is a sort of confidence that this will one day make sense in the light of the whole pattern of Hebrew prophecy – but it is not quite there yet. The Easter event was new enough, strange enough and worrying enough not to have any ready-made structure for it. In spite of the prophecies that Jesus himself is said to have uttered about it (8.31, 9.31, 10.34), it still comes to his followers as a surprise, as though the sheer brute fact of his humiliating death had obliterated any memory of any hope expressed by Jesus.

And then there are those who maintain that it's just an accident that the Gospel ends where and as it does: the last page was lost and never rediscovered (as if there was only one copy in circulation?) or, as the great New Testament interpreter and scholar Austin Farrer mischievously put it, that a heavy hand descended on Mark's shoulder as he wrote 16.8, and a centurion's voice said, 'I'm afraid I'll have to ask you to come along with me to the Praetorium.' With Farrer, I am inclined to think that the accident theory does far less than justice to a writer of real subtlety. A surprising ending is perhaps in tune with a text that has all the way through been preparing us to be surprised. If the ending were more conventional, like the endings added by later hands, it would not have carried the force it does in the light of all that has gone before.

The text as it stands tells us that speaking about faith will never be easy, because, when the first announcement of the truth was made, the witnesses couldn't cope. Just as with the stupidity of the apostles throughout the Gospel, the reader's own bewilderment and incomprehension is signalled in advance. Don't be surprised if you can't manage to get your head around this: it always was this way. Mark is a book that tells you how hard it is to read and so tells you to give it the time it needs. It may be short, and it may be short on detail, but it takes as long as it takes to read, because you will never have finished it. You will have to go over and over again to rediscover the possibilities of trust and faith in the helpless, powerless God. And in that process, you will find that what Jesus speaks of in chapter 10 – the absolute centrality of service, of self-gift, not of secure control over others – is what begins to come alive in your reading and your responding.

I mentioned briefly a moment ago the way that Mark uses allusions to the Old Testament. He quotes Isaiah a great deal and a certain amount from the Psalms quite a bit, with scattered references to the Law of Moses and one or two of the other prophets. Here, as in the other Gospels – though rather less so than in St Matthew, for example – the point is that when you have grasped the revolutionary strangeness of what's going on in Jesus, there is also a moment of realizing '. . . but of course, if we had only known how to read the whole history of God's work in Creation and in his relation with Israel, we'd have seen this was natural'. This of course is the theme which St Luke spells out for us in the story of the risen Jesus meeting two disciples on the road to Emmaus. Jesus says (Luke 24.25–26) to the disciples, 'You are so stupid and sluggish in your hearts! Wasn't it clearly necessary for the Anointed to suffer?' Mark is already preparing us for that kind of realization. We can now look back on the whole range and record of God's work and see that, after all, yes, this was to be expected had we only been able to read the clues. When we grasp that the God who is present in and as Jesus is after all the same God who has been at work throughout, we can begin to piece together the full picture. It's a kind of 'double vision' very typical of the

New Testament. Nothing could have prepared us for what was going on in the death of Jesus and everything should have prepared us for it.

Looking at the overall patterns of Mark's text, we can see that it is a book about how Jesus – the reality of Jesus in his own history and the continuing reality of Jesus in his community – takes you constantly in and out of silence, in and out of language. Here for a moment you see, you grasp; and you then have to let go and begin again. You think that you might have mastered it; and suddenly find you haven't, and you must be quiet and listen. This Gospel is a book about faith, and more specifically about that fundamental aspect of faith which is the trustful letting go into a love that is completely surprising and works completely by its own rules, not yours. That perhaps is why it's appropriate to think of Mark – whether he was the first of the Evangelists or not – as in a strong sense the 'beginning' of the gospel and the 'first principle' of the gospel (the Greek word *arche* has both meanings): the place where the distinctive colour of the Christian faith is defined.

Of course Mark doesn't say everything. The most closely related Gospels, Matthew and Luke, have essential things to say about Jesus and about us. Both have the stories of Jesus' birth and childhood. Matthew has the Sermon on the Mount and works with a powerful stress on continuity: Jesus is truly the climax of all God's working in the history of Israel. He spells out the story of Jesus as both the natural culmination of all God's work and a drastically new phase, a new perspective. It is not at all a perspective alien to Mark, except that he does it through the words, through the teaching of Jesus, rather than simply in the stark emphasis on the lonely dereliction of Jesus. Matthew is more of an historian in a sense that his narrative has a beginning and an end and a touch of order within it; and the price paid is that his narrative is that little bit more domesticated and less disturbing. Luke too has the teaching discourses, but adds to them the great parables of Jesus – the Prodigal Son and the Good Samaritan and others. Luke has probably the most warming and appealing portrait of a Jesus whose embrace for the outcast and the forgotten is at the centre of his compelling authority; for most Christians, Luke is the most accessible and the best loved of the Gospels, its stories the most quoted. Luke spells out the same inversion of the world's values that Mark alerts us to, but does so in terms of Jesus' embrace of the stranger, the foreigner, the failure; and, like Matthew but even more so, he does it with a careful style and an elegant narrative structure.

Yet Mark is in some ways the bedrock of it all. Strangely, he is in many respects more like John than he is like Matthew or Luke. Like John, he begins with a declaration of something completely radical, grounded in the heavenly places; his text begins and ends in mystery. Like John, he has at the heart of his narrative Jesus' self-identification by the words, 'I am.' Like John he ends with a teasing and inconclusive moment: John (21.25) by saying that it would be impossible to write all that Jesus did because the world would not be able to contain it. What Jesus did and does has no end, and certainly not in the pages of a book, because the work he does he is doing in every new reader, and there will always be new readers. That is not at all unlike Mark in relation to what we have seen to be implied in the way he ends: it's for us to decide whether we become part of that process of spreading the word of the resurrection that the women at first are too frightened to. The work of Jesus in the reader is the 'end' of the Gospel.

So unless we grasp that dimension of Mark that leads into silence and bewilderment, there's something we shall miss about the whole revolution in values and visions that he articulates for us. We shall miss the radical depth of the new world of the kingdom, the newness of the Good News. Mark is not the whole gospel, but it makes sense to read him as the beginning of the gospel and the 'first principle' of the gospel, pointing us to something foundational. If this reading is right, it is anything but a naïve work; it is not a simple affair of gathering community traditions and threading them together in a somewhat haphazard way. Nor is it an 'edifying' work, teaching us good behaviour through uplifting teaching and improving thoughts. It is a book which repeats on every page that summons to *metanoia*, to a change of mind, that Jesus demands of his hearers in the first words he utters in the text.

There is one last thought, perhaps somewhat fanciful but not idle. We have looked at the ancient tradition that Peter stands behind the writing of the Gospel of Mark; and, as I have indicated, I believe there may be more to be said for this than some recent generations of scholars have allowed. But there is surely a deeper level at which Peter is indeed the key figure of the Gospel in relation to how we think about the hearers and followers of Jesus. The Peter of St Mark is not a prince of the apostles, sovereignly getting his answers right time after time. He is rather the typical hearer of Jesus, the typical witness; and the typical witness for Mark is the one who repeatedly misses the point of what is witnessed, the one who most unequivocally gets it wrong time after time, yet is still held by the questioning eyes of Jesus. Peter's exemplary wrongness is nowhere more hideously in evidence than at the moment of his denial: at exactly the moment when God is declaring himself in Jesus' 'I am' in reply to the High Priest's question, Peter, answering someone else's question a few yards away, is literally saying, 'I am not.' The fullness of truth in the helpless and rejected Jesus has its negative image in the emptiness of Peter's evasion.

Peter stands for all the human characters whom Jesus confronts – the apostles, the witnesses, the Church, ourselves.

He is us; brought to nothing by his inability to hear and receive the transfiguring presence of God in the helpless and condemned Jesus, but called afresh out of his own chaos to the task of finding words for the mystery. Perhaps it really is after all the Gospel of Peter; and if it is the Gospel of Peter, we can be sure it is the gospel for all of us.

Questions for reflection or group discussion

1 The beginning of the Gospel

1 If you came across a pamphlet or book called *Good News*, what would you expect to find inside?

2 How would the proclamation of Mark 1.14 sound in your own words?

3 What difference does it make, in your experience of the text, to know who Mark was and why he wrote this Gospel? Does Mark's distance from Jesus or the timing of his writing affect the value you find in this Gospel?

4 What would it be like to have a relationship with a Fr Philemon-type figure – or Jesus himself – so compelling that concern for whether his miraculous acts 'really happened' fades away? What does it feel like for scepticism to give way to something deeper?

5 Compare the opening paragraphs of Matthew, Mark, Luke and John. What do you think about the difference between Mark's introduction and those of the other Gospel writers?

2 Telling secrets

1 What is your response when someone asks you to keep something significant a secret? Does this same reaction hold true when it is Jesus asking for secrecy? Why do you think Jesus wants to keep his specialness under wraps?

2 How would Mark's Gospel (and the broader 'good news' of Jesus) be different if Jesus hadn't behaved in such strange and superhuman ways? Given the presence of other charismatic healers and teachers in Jesus' day, how did his behaviour and style set him apart?

3 What does the saying, 'Lord, I believe. Help my unbelief', mean to you? Is this a prayer you can identify with?

4 Do Jesus' parables make sense to you? Do you think his refusal to explain them or his claim of not wanting people to understand is a mode of secrecy or a challenge to think deeply?

5 How do you envisage God's working in you? Do you see God above and beyond you, reaching into your heart and life, or 'outward from the heart of being into the life of every day'? How would this inside-out perspective change the way you experience God and live your faith in the world?

3 A lifelong passion

1 What do you think is the power of place? Do you find significance in pondering the location of certain events?

2 Emphasizing Jesus' solitude and powerlessness during the Passion, as Mark does, can make Jesus easier to relate to than in those Gospels where the writers consistently remind the readers of the possibility of God's intervention. Does Mark's approach enhance your experience of God through Jesus' story, or does it cause you to doubt and fear?

3 What do you see as the significance of Jesus' death in our salvation? Does the idea of God – the great 'I AM' – being fully present with the victimized, suffering and abandoned have a merely comforting or truly salvific effect?

4 The ransom theory of atonement, suggested in Mark 10.45, is one of numerous hypotheses about how, exactly, Jesus' death saves humankind. What does this theory – indicating that Jesus' life is the fee demanded by a kidnapper in exchange for our souls – suggest about God's power?

5 The ending to Mark's Gospel is mysterious, especially when compared to the other Gospel writers' accounts. Does this abrupt ending cast doubt on the resurrection for you or add power to the story, no matter how you might envisage what follows?

Lenten reading guide

Week one

(Ash Wednesday to the First Sunday of Lent)

Wednesday:	Mark 1.1–13
Thursday:	Mark 1.14–28
Friday:	Mark 1.29–45
Saturday:	Mark 2.1–17

Sunday reflection

Unlike the other Gospels, Mark jumps right into Jesus' adult life and ministry, with his baptism by John, temptation in the wilderness, calling of the first disciples and numerous healings. The 62 verses read this week offer an intense, close-up view of Jesus' early ministry. If these passages were all you knew of the Jesus story, what would your reaction be? Try to imagine yourself hearing this bit of 'good news' for the first time, and encountering Jesus afresh, without the baggage of centuries of conflict and myriad interpretations. Let the story of Jesus surprise and amaze you.

God, grant me fresh eyes to see Jesus like one of those first receiving the good news. Amen.

Week two

Monday:	Mark 2.18–28
Tuesday:	Mark 3.1–12
Wednesday:	Mark 3.13–35
Thursday:	Mark 4.1–20
Friday:	Mark 4.21–34
Saturday:	Mark 4.35–41

Sunday reflection

Jesus was a controversial figure, and sometimes a confusing one. He plucked grain on the Sabbath, which was unlawful but not unprecedented. His own family said he was out of his mind and must have a demon. He told cryptic stories but wouldn't explain them, except to his disciples. He healed without even a touch and calmed a raging storm with a simple rebuke. What is your reaction to these stories? Does it make a difference to you whether these events happened just as Mark says? What impression do these stories give you of Jesus, and how do you experience God through them?

God, let me stand in awe of your power. Give me wonder that goes beyond fact and fiction. Amen.

Week three

Monday:	Mark 5.1–20
Tuesday:	Mark 5.21–43
Wednesday:	Mark 6.1–13
Thursday:	Mark 6.14–29

| Friday: | Mark 6.30–56 |
| Saturday: | Mark 7.1–23 |

Sunday reflection

Reactions to Jesus (and similarly, John, in the middle of chapter 6) vary widely, from awe and enthusiasm to contempt and violent rejection. What distinctions do you see between those who are eager to see, hear and touch these holy men and those who condemn them? We all like to think we would have embraced Jesus enthusiastically and looked to him for wisdom and healing, but might we have been among his opponents? What do you have in common with those who embraced Jesus, and what do you have in common with those who rejected him?

God, grant me the humility to see my own privilege. Let me see Jesus' challenge as a gift and not a threat. Amen.

Week four

Monday:	Mark 7.24–37
Tuesday:	Mark 8.1–21
Wednesday:	Mark 8.22—9.1
Thursday:	Mark 9.2–29
Friday:	Mark 9.30–50
Saturday:	Mark 10.1–16

Sunday reflection

The stakes seem to grow higher as Jesus gets deeper into his public ministry. He seems to get easily frustrated, dismissing a Syro-Phoenician woman who asks for help and walking away from

Pharisees who ask for a sign. He shames disciples who don't seem to 'get it', but sternly orders those who do proclaim his identity to keep quiet about it. Combined with Jesus' discussion of his coming death, bold display on the mountaintop, and affirmation of those outside the disciples' circle, what do you think is behind Jesus' attitude in these chapters? Why do you think Mark portrayed Jesus this way, even if his writing would make readers confused by or concerned about Jesus?

God, help me to walk in Jesus' shoes and experience the world through his eyes as we approach the time of his trial and death. Amen.

Week five

Monday:	Mark 10.17–34
Tuesday:	Mark 10.35–52
Wednesday:	Mark 11.1–11
Thursday:	Mark 11.12–33
Friday:	Mark 12.1–17
Saturday:	Mark 12.18–37

Sunday reflection

Some people dismiss Lent as a depressing time of unnecessary, self-imposed suffering. Reflect on your own experience of self-denial and also on struggles people endure by sheer accident or misfortune. Consider these things in the light of Jesus' teachings about the blessedness of those who are not rich, who have left home and family to follow him, and who take on the role of servant to others. Do your ideas of who is blessed in the world align with Jesus'? How do these teachings challenge you to live differently, not just during Lent but throughout the year?

God, help me to see my own struggles and those of others through your eyes. Transform my desire for success and satisfaction into a desire to please you. Amen.

Week six

Monday:	Mark 12.38–44
Tuesday:	Mark 13.1–23
Wednesday:	Mark 13.24–37
Thursday:	Mark 14.1–11
Friday:	Mark 14.12–31
Saturday:	Mark 14.32–52

Sunday reflection

From Jesus' teaching in the Temple to his dramatic arrest in the garden, the tension between Jesus and the authorities is building, as is the reader's sense of agitation. Jesus is becoming more isolated, and even his followers' efforts at faithfulness are found wanting. As readers, our enthusiasm for this climax to Jesus' story is tempered by his unsettling apocalyptic warnings. What do you imagine God is experiencing as the time of the Son's death draws near? How would you feel if you were one of Jesus' disciples at this stage of his ministry?

God, give me insight to experience Jesus' story as it was, not only the beautiful parts, but the difficult as well. Amen.

Week seven

Monday:	Mark 14.53–72
Tuesday:	Mark 15.1–20
Wednesday:	Mark 15.21–39
Thursday:	Mark 15.40–47
Friday:	Mark 16.1–8a
Saturday:	Mark 16.8b–20

Sunday reflection

The ending of Mark's Gospel is notable largely for what it doesn't say. Jesus' near-total silence during his trial and crucifixion emphasizes the mood of resignation and despair, and the seeming prematurity of the book's original ending adds mystery as well as anticipation. This strikes some readers as powerful and evocative while causing confusion and scepticism in others. Imagine you were alive in the second century and considering conversion to Christianity: what effect would Mark's points of silence have on you? As a modern follower of Jesus celebrating Easter Sunday, what impact do accounts of Jesus' resurrection appearances have on you?

God, thank you for Jesus' triumph over death. Thank you for the writers who passed down the good news of Jesus, each in their own way. Amen.

Notes

1 Jürgen Moltmann, *A Broad Place: An autobiography* (London, SCM Press, 2007), p. 30.

2 Gillian Crow, *'This Holy Man'. Impressions of Metropolitan Anthony* (London, Darton, Longman and Todd, 2005), p. 41.

3 Charles Williams, *He Came Down from Heaven* (London, Heinemann, 1938), p. 60.

4 Williams, *He Came Down from Heaven*, p. 63.

5 James M. Robinson (ed.), *The Nag Hammadi Library in English* (Leiden, E. J. Brill, 1977), p. 130.

6 The classic version of this argument can be found in Etienne Trocmé, *The Passion as Liturgy: A study in the origin of the Passion narratives in the four Gospels* (London, SCM Press, 1983).

7 Trocmé, *The Passion as Liturgy*, p. 79.

Suggestions for further reading

Raymond Brown, *An Introduction to the New Testament* (New York, Doubleday, 1996), pp. 126–70.
A magisterial summary of scholarly debate, very clearly presented.

Richard Burridge, *Four Gospels, One Jesus: A symbolic reading* (London, SPCK, 2013).
A very readable and imaginative survey of how the Gospel narratives work.

Morna D. Hooker, *The Gospel according to St Mark* (London, A&C Black, 1991).
One of the best modern commentaries.

Leslie Houlden, *The Strange Story of the Gospels: Finding doctrine through narrative* (London, SPCK, 2002).
Original and searching reflections on the diverse styles of Christian identity and discipleship represented by the Gospel writers through their methods of storytelling.

Luke Timothy Johnson, *The Real Jesus: The misguided quest for the historical Jesus and the truth of the traditional Gospels* (San Francisco, HarperCollins, 1996).
A challenge to some modern attempts to recover a Jesus 'before' the Gospels.

Ched Myers, *Binding the Strong Man: A political reading of Mark's story of Jesus* (New York, Orbis, 2008, 2nd edn).
The most authoritative picture of Mark's text in its historical and social setting.

David Rhoads, Joanna Dewey and Donald Michie, *Mark as Story: An introduction to the narrative of a Gospel* (Philadelphia, Fortress Press, 2012, 3rd edn).
Ground-breaking analysis of Mark's literary technique.

CPSIA information can be obtained
at www.ICGtesting.com
Printed in the USA
FFOW01n0636210115
10470FF